THEN SINGS MY SOUL

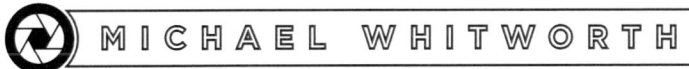
MICHAEL WHITWORTH

A DECADE OF UNSEEN GRACE

Ten years of mornings.
Ten years of waking before the world stirred,
chasing a vision only my soul could see—
a moment of perfect light
kissing the spires of Bryce
just as heaven opens its eyes.

I returned again and again,
boots crunching frost,
hands numb around the same old camera,
sky too cloudy, light too dull,
or beauty just beyond what I could frame.

And with every not-quite,
I wondered:
Was it foolish?
Was I missing the mark—or missing the point?

But still, I came.
Not because I believed in my skill,
but because something holy whispered,
"Return. Wait. Watch."

Sunrise on Thor's Hammer
Bryce Canyon National Park

Year after year,
I stood in silence with hopes unmet,
yet somehow full—
because even failure, when held with faith,
becomes a form of prayer.

And then—
one morning not unlike the rest,
with no sign, no promise—
the canyon bloomed in fire and gold.
Light poured like grace between stone fingers,
and I, too, was lit from within.

I pressed the shutter.
I captured the frame.
But it was not the image that broke me open;
it was the journey to it.

Because now I know:
the gift was never just the photograph.
It was what God carved in me
through all the trying.

The patience shaped me.
The returning refined me.
The empty hands taught me how to receive.

And when the light finally came,
I was ready to see more than just beauty—
I saw mercy.
I saw presence.
I saw a decade of unseen grace
woven through the waiting.

So now I tell you:
Don't despise the slow climb,
the unopened doors,
the prayers answered in silence.

For even when the goal is far,
the effort is never wasted.
You are being drawn,
reshaped,
readied.

And when your moment comes—
as it surely will—
you'll find that the breakthrough
was not just in what you captured,
but in who you became while reaching for it.

GLORY AT LAST LIGHT

I came expecting glory—
painted skies and fire-streaked stone,
a masterpiece descending in full view.
But the heavens were cloaked in slate,
thick with silence,
clouds heavy with indifference.

No color.
No drama.
Just a dull, gray hush
settling over the canyon's open wound.

And I sighed—
another sunset missed,
another moment lost
to the weight of waiting and hope deferred.

But then—
as if Heaven had been hiding on purpose—
the edge of the world caught flame.

Not loud.
Not sweeping.
But sure.

A thin ribbon of light,
blazing just above the horizon,
as if God had parted the veil
for a single, holy breath.

And I stood still—
no longer disappointed,
but undone.
Because the glory had always been coming—
I just didn't know it would wait
until the very end.

That sliver of sunset
was more than light—
it was a promise:

Even on the cloudiest days,
when beauty feels impossible,
and joy hides behind the weight of what hasn't come,
God is still moving.

Sometimes, he saves the brilliance
for the moment we almost give up,
just to show us—
He was never late.
Just waiting
for our hearts to be still enough to see.

So now, I remember:
When life is overcast,
when prayers echo in fog,
when disappointment dulls the soul—
hold on.

Because even in the last breath of day,
the light can break through.
And when it does,
it speaks louder than any perfect sky:

"I am still here. I never left. And I am more beautiful than you dared to hope."

Dusk on the Dunes
White Sands National Park

IN THE SILENCE, I AM SEEN

I walked the waves of silent white,
where dunes rise like breath held in prayer,
and the sun spills gold on every crest.
So many grains beneath my feet—
countless, shifting, shimmering bright—
yet none lost to the gaze of God.

Each one, a whisper of time,
a fragment of earth's ancient song,
carried here by wind and will,
resting now in sacred stillness.
They seem the same—
but no two grains wear the same face,
no two reflect the light quite alike.

And it strikes me:
If God can know each grain,
can count them, name them,
trace the journey of each tiny wanderer,
then how much more
am I seen?

Not lost in the sea of souls,
not just one among billions,
but shaped, noticed,
known—like sand in his palm.

Here, where silence hums eternity,
I feel the nearness of the infinite.
In the quiet,
even the smallest things are holy.

ETERNITY CHANGES ITS FACE

I return again, as I always do
to the edge of this breathless stillness,
where the world falls away into forever,
and the river cuts time in stone.

Each visit feels like the first and the last.
No two skies ever wear the same robe.
One morning, the cliffs are crimson prayers;
the next they're silent ghosts in fog.

Shadows stretch differently with each season's hand,
curling around buttes like sacred verses—
Winter's hush, Summer's thundered blaze,
Autumn's gold, Spring's whispered promise.

The light—oh, the light!
It dances, it lingers, it reveals what once was hidden:
A crack becomes a canyon,
a stone becomes a shrine.

I do not grow tired.
Because this place is not still—it is becoming.
Just like me.
We are both carved by the same unseen wind.

So I come back, again and again,
not to see the same—but to be changed.
For in every glance across that endless space,
I glimpse eternity wearing a different face.

Green River Overlook
Canyonlands National Park

GLORY IN THE BROKEN PLACES
(A Father's Day hymn to the tune of *Come Thou Fount*)

Lord of sorrow, Lord of splendor,
In the hush of grief I came—
Carved by loss and long surrender,
Bearing wounds I could not name.
Years had passed, and still the aching
Echoed deep within my soul,
Yet you led me, gently waking
Hope where once was an empty soul.

Father's Day—the ache returning,
Two great loves no longer near,
Still my spirit kept on yearning
For a glimpse that you were near.
Not in grand design I found it,
Not in answers, swift and clear,
But in stillness, you surrounded
Me with glory drawing near.

There it was—your light, unbidden,
Moraine's mirror, calm and wide—
Clouds had lifted, beauty hidden
Now displayed in holy pride.
I raised my lens, but more—my spirit,
Caught in awe, began to sing.
Worship rose, and I could hear it—
Heaven's hush in everything.

So it is with pain and glory—
Grief and wonder interlace.
You still write a greater story
In the harshest, barren place.
Loss remains, yet love grows deeper,
For you meet me where I stand—
Not with answers, but the Keeper
Holding sorrow in his hand.

Let this picture now remind me,
When the days are dark and long—
You still come, and you still find me,
Filling silence with your song.
Unexpected, undeserving,
You reveal what eyes can't see—
God of mercy, ever serving,
Bringing glory back to me.

Moraine Lake
Banff National Park

LITURGY OF LIGHT

Before the light, the land lay still—
A cathedral carved by time and silence.
Stone upon stone, ancient and waiting,
Holding its breath beneath a brooding sky.
The river curled through shadow below,
A silver thread in the canyon's hand,
As if it, too, waited
For something more than morning.

And then—
The first light came.

Not loud. Not rushing.
But sure.
Golden and soft as breath,
It kissed the rim of the world—
And suddenly, the canyon caught fire.

Layer by layer, wall by wall,
Light descended in sacred waves.
It spilled across the red rock spires,
Lit mesas like altars,
And draped the cliffs in robes of flame.

Even the silence changed.
It felt holy now—
Like something ancient had awakened,
Or Someone had walked through the stillness
And left glory behind.

Sunrise at Dead Horse Point (previous page)
Dead Horse Point State Park

O God—
What kind of hand paints with such fire?
What kind of mind imagines this depth?
This wilderness of wonder
Is not just landscape—
It is liturgy.
It is You.

You come like morning over desert stone—
Steady, sweeping, all-consuming.
You touch what was barren,
You reveal what was hidden,
You break open the dark
Not with noise,
But with glory.

And I—
I am undone.

For this canyon is not the only thing You flood.
You pour into the soul just the same—
Layer by layer,
Shadow by shadow,
Until the heart becomes
A place of praise.

I came to witness beauty,
But I leave having encountered God.
Not in thunder,
But in light.
Not in answer,
But in awe.

Let this sunrise be a promise:
That no matter how deep the valley,
Or long the night,
The light will come—
And when it does,
It will touch everything.

Milky Way over Bryce Amphitheater
Bryce Canyon National Park

LORD OF THE NIGHT SKIES
(to the tune of *In Christ Alone*)

O Lord of light, whose voice has sown
The stars that crown your midnight throne.
From Milky Way to mountains' crest,
Your glory shines; your works confess.
Each gleaming spark declares your Name.
Through depths of night your pow'r remains.
The heavens sing, creation cries:
"All praise to you, Lord of the skies."

You shaped the night, yet know my way;
Your hand still turns my dark to day.
The galaxies in silence turn
While hearts of clay your mercies learn.
From dusk to dawn your wonders call,
Your steadfast love upholds it all.
The heavens tell what words can't say.
Our Maker speaks, and stars obey.

The stars proclaim your endless might,
Each shining world beyond our sight.
Yet in your grace you stoop to hear
The cries of faith that pierce the night.
The heavens span eternity
Yet still your love remembers me.
Though small beneath the vast unknown,
You claim my heart to be your own.

Milky Way over The Watchman
Zion National Park

OUR GOD, HIS WONDERS SING
(to the tune of *Our God, He Is Alive*)

The morning breaks with crimson fire,
The eastern skies proclaim his name.
Each sunrise speaks of his desire
To light our hearts with holy flame.

The setting sun with golden rays
Spreads glory through the quiet skies.
The painted clouds in evening's haze
Reveal the work of One all-wise.

At night, the stars in silence sing,
The Milky Way stretched high and wide.
A glimpse of heaven's reigning King,
Whose power no darkness can hide.

His wonders shine on land and sea,
In desert winds and forests tall.
The skies declare his majesty—
Our God, the Maker rules them all.

Milky Way over Mesa Arch
Canyonlands National Park

Milky Way over Mount Hood
Lost Lake, Oregon

Milky Way over Balanced Rock
Arches National Park

MOUNTAINS THAT PREACH

In silence high, the mountains rise,
Their heads adorned with sapphire skies.
Majestic walls of stone and grace,
They hold the echoes of God's face.

Each peak a hymn, each ridge a psalm,
In roaring winds or stillness calm.
They preach without a single word—
Yet in their might, His voice is heard.

Their roots go deep where secrets sleep,
Where ancient prayers the shadows keep.
And snow that crowns their ageless brow
Still bows to Him in silent vow.

The thunder rolls across their spines,
Like heaven's drum in sacred lines.
The stars lean close, the eagles soar—
Creation calls: "Come, praise the Lord!"

No temple built by human hand
Could match what here in silence stands.
These towers born of earth and flame
Now lift the glory of His name.

So when I stand beneath their height,
I glimpse His power, feel His light.
And in their strength and sacred sod,
I see the fingerprints of God.

Dawn at Reflection Pond
Mount Rainier National Park

Two Jack Lake (next page)
Banff National Park

Peyto Lake
Banff National Park

HOLY ABOVE THE HEIGHTS

Holy, holy, holy! In the heights I find you—
Every peak and pathway draws my soul in prayer.
Lifted by the silence, heaven seems to shine through,
Whispering gently: "Child, know I am here."

Holy, holy, holy! Mountains stand before me,
Timeless, firm, and faithful—like your love and grace.
In their mighty stillness, I behold your glory,
And feel your nearness fill this sacred place.

Holy, holy, holy! When the clouds enfold them,
Still I sense your presence walking on the wind.
Even in the shadows, I am not forsaken—
Here in the highlands, I know you again.

Holy, holy, holy! Maker of the mountains,
You who carved the valleys, raised the skies above—
Here I lift my heart up, drinking from your fountain,
Held in your wonder, resting in your love.

IN THE RIGHT LIGHT

There are mornings when the hills wear a veil,
a quiet mist that refuses to be hurried.
The patient photographer stands at the fence-line,
boots dark with dew, breath rising like prayer.
He cannot tug the sun into place
or command the clouds to part;
he can only keep watch,
trusting the world will open in its time.

So it is with the soul.

We come to the same ridge of Scripture,
the same ancient promises,
again and again—
sometimes catching only silhouettes,
sometimes a faint glimmer on the far horizon.
We wait, and the waiting feels wasteful
until the Spirit reminds us
that stillness is its own obedience,
that wisdom rarely shouts,
that revelation is more dawn than lightning.

The seasoned photographer knows
the landscape is always speaking,
even when the light is wrong.
He studies its contours,
walks its winding ridges,
memorizes the lines of its rivers,
learning how beauty hides
and when it is likely to appear.
He returns in winter,
in the slow green of spring,
in the fragile blush of autumn—
not to force a moment,
but to be present when it comes.

This, too, is spiritual formation.

Storm over the Tetons
Grand Teton National Park

We cannot manufacture understanding.
We can only kneel in the places
where grace has visited before—
open Bible, open heart,
hands unclenched,
eyes attentive to the slightest clearing.
We come in seasons of joy,
in times of hunger,
in the long stretch of unanswered prayers.
We come because light has a way
of keeping appointments with those
who refuse to leave.

The prophets whisper this truth:
those who wait on the Lord
rise not by effort but by promise.
Strength does not bloom in frantic hearts
but in those who hold their ground
beneath an unhurried sky.
And James tells us
wisdom descends like a gift,
not wrestled from heaven
but given to the ones
who keep showing up with empty hands.

So we practice holy patience.
We linger at the edge of mystery.
We learn the cadence of God's appearing,
how he often arrives quietly—
not with spectacle,
but with the still, sure light
that slips between clouds
when we least expect it.

And one day—
after many dawns that offered nothing,
after evenings spent in fading hope—
the veil lifts.

The valley fills with radiance.
Details we never noticed
burn with clarity:
the curve of mercy in our failures,
the shimmer of grace along old wounds,
the steadfast contours of a God
who never stopped shaping us
in the shadows.

We lift the camera—
or the heart—
and receive what we could never create.

For holiness, like perfect light,
is always a gift.
And those who wait
discover what the patient know:
that the right light always comes,
and always in its time.

Snow & First Light (next page)
Crater Lake National Park

THE ROCK THAT HOLDS THE NIGHT

No matter how dark the night becomes,
or how the winds unnerve my bones,
i lift my eyes and find you still—
big and strong and steady as stone.

The world may tremble at the edges,
shadows may stretch far and deep,
but you stand sure as a mountain peak,
holding my fear while i learn to breathe.

Night cannot shrink the truth of you;
darkness cannot make you small.
You are the quiet strength that stays—
the solid ground beneath it all.

Trillium Lake
Government Camp, Oregon

www.ingramcontent.com/pod-product-compliance
Lightning Source LLC
Chambersburg PA
CBRC090450090526
44586CB00032BA/91